Looking at pictures
in the Tate Gallery
with Michael Compton

THE TATE GALLERY

ISBN 0 905005 61 9
Published by order of the Trustees 1979
Copyright © 1979 The Tate Gallery
Designed by Sue Fowler
Published by the Tate Gallery Publications Department,
Millbank, London SW1 4RG
Printed in Great Britain by Balding & Mansell, Wisbech, Cambs.

Introduction

The Tate Gallery is the home of our country's collection of British Art and of Modern Art from all over the western world. Paintings, sculptures, drawings and prints are kept here for everyone to see. Many of our visitors come again and again but we are specially pleased to have new visitors so that we can show them things that they have not seen before, things that they may come to love or find exciting.

One of the purposes of art is to give us experiences and understanding that we cannot always find in our ordinary lives. We can learn how people looked and behaved in the past, and about what they thought most important. We can be shown that things can be beautiful or exciting in ways that we had never noticed before. We can understand better how people make sense of all the variety of shapes and colours that they see from moment to moment and how they react to these and use them in order to live in the world.

Nobody can expect to understand everything about a picture and no one needs to like all works of art. Artists are people who constantly look for what has not been seen, felt or understood before and for ways of presenting what they find in paintings, drawings or sculpture. It may take people some time to catch up with what they have done.

If you are interested in new things and new ideas, or if you like looking at pictures but do not know much about art, this book may help you get more out of a visit to the Tate Gallery. It also tries to show how each of the many different kinds of art has its own value both to people in its own day and to us now.

I have chosen some pictures and sculptures in the Tate which show the enormous variety of ways in which artists have worked and the different ways they have represented the world, their thoughts and feelings. In each one I have tried to point out some things that you might not notice and to explain others that you may not understand or that you may not see the purpose of. As well as writing about the picture or sculpture itself, I have tried to use it to bring out something that is typical of its period or which may be found in paintings of many periods.

The paintings and sculptures are shown more or less in the order of date in which they were made. This gives an idea of the way art has changed as each artist has built on the inventions of those that went before and as the world in which they work has developed.

At the back of the book you will find pages that deal with topics that are common to almost all works of art, what they are made of and some of the methods artists use. These are related by notes in brackets to the particular pictures and sculptures at the front. Sometimes you will find a further explanation at the back of a complicated matter that is mentioned briefly in the description of one of the works at the front.

The order in which the works are described is also the order in which they are generally shown in the Tate Gallery itself. The British paintings from about 1500 to 1900 are on the left side of the building as you go into it, and the modern paintings and sculptures on the right. Straight ahead you will usually find exhibitions of works of art lent to the Gallery so that you can see the whole of what an individual artist achieved, or in much more detail, how some kind of art developed and what it was like.

If you find this book interesting and want to know more about the works of the art in the Tate and others like them, you can read a longer account in the Gallery's illustrated companion. This can be found in the Gallery shop which sells many helpful books, as well as postcards and reproductions of many of the pictures, so that you can keep a reminder of the works of art you have liked.

Every day there are tours of the parts of the Gallery given by people who can tell you about the works or help you to understand them more fully. Many parties come from schools and we will always arrange for someone to introduce the Gallery and its collections to a class or other group of people if they let us know they want to come.

In the entrance there is an information desk where there are always people who can answer questions about the Tate and what is in it. The men and women in uniform who stand in the galleries are there mainly to protect the works of art but they will be pleased to help you find anything you want to see.

So this book is only one way in which we can help you to enjoy the marvellous paintings and sculptures that we keep for the nation in the Tate Gallery.

It is open almost every day of the year to visit without charge and we hope you will come to see what we have if you have not been before. If you have, you will certainly find new things every time you come again and new ways of looking at things you have seen before.

Note. The dimensions are given in centimetres; height precedes width and in the case of sculpture, the last figure is depth.

The Cholmondeley Sisters

This picture must have been painted to commemorate the unusual event described in the writing which is on it. Pictures often tell you about people and life in the past.

Although we call the two ladies 'sisters', the writing does not say so. They might have been cousins, for example, but they were certainly not identical twins. If you look closely you can see that the lady on the left has blue eyes and the one on the right brown. Each baby has eyes of the same colour as its mother and is wearing the same material on the front of its dress as she does, so the family connection is clearly brought out.

The picture seems to record the christening of the babies. This usually happened soon after they were born because so many babies died very young. They are wrapped in their christening robes and their mothers are wearing decorative hoods, which you can see above their big ruff collars. These would have been worn for the ceremony. The clothes may seem much too stiff and complicated for anyone to wear in bed, but on all occasions and especially on those that marked important family and public events, people wore clothes that indicated their place in society. This tradition still exists in the army, for example, but in those days it affected almost everybody and a painter would have to be very careful to represent the clothes accurately.

In our picture the clothes seem almost more important than the people wearing them. The ladies are not shown as individuals but as members of their family and rank in society. We are not told their names. They are dressed almost exactly alike, and they are even sitting holding their babies in exactly the same position, one that you can see in other pictures of mothers of the same period.

In fact the picture is not very natural, as you can tell by comparing it to the next one in this book. Like other portraits of its day it did not need to be very natural. Portraits were the most usual kind of pictures. They were often hung up in large numbers in a special room, called the gallery, of the great houses of the aristocrats and large landowners to show off the superiority of their family and political connections. Clothes and other indications of rank and wealth were therefore more important than naturalness.

Like other paintings of the period 'The Cholmondeley Sisters' was painted to satisfy the client rather than the artist – he was paid to produce only what his client wanted. Some painters were very famous for their skill but others like this one were local craftsmen and we do not even know his name.

British School 17th Century
The Cholmondeley Sisters *c*.1600–10
Oil on wood, 88.9 x 172.7

left
Detail of the writing which describes
the event illustrated in the painting

The Graham Children

This is a picture of the four children of the apothecary of the Chelsea Hospital. Although the word 'apothecary' means more or less the same as 'chemist', Mr Graham was in charge of the medical treatment of the patients in the hospital. The post and its salary was inherited by the little boy on the right when he was only about fourteen so he must have employed others to do the real work.

Hogarth's friends and the people he painted for were generally of this kind of middle rank in society, professionals and businessmen rather than aristocrats and landowners like the Cholmondeleys. Although family connections remained important, a person's individual abilities counted much more among them and that is one of the reasons why the picture seems a great deal more natural. The faces have individual expressions and each child is shown doing something different.

The children seem to be in a real, though rather grand, room; in fact it is grander than Mr Graham's own room which, I believe, had an ordinary wooden floor. Hogarth has painted a black and white marble floor, like a chess board. One of its functions is to make clear how the figures are arranged in the space of the room. The three girls stand more or less on the diagonal black squares while the boy has his feet on the white square near the middle of the space left over. This is one way in which the boy, who is about nine in the picture, is singled out from his sisters by the artist. The boy is also the most active one. He is working a kind of music box

that imitates bird calls and is looking at the bird in the cage to see what happens.

In fact the picture tells you something of what people believed about how children grow up and how they would be expected to behave. The baby is interested in nothing but food; the young girl is playing unselfconsciously at being a lady at a dance; while the older girl looks out shyly at you for she is beginning to realise she is a woman. On the other hand the boy is experimenting with a mechanical device.

The cat on the right and the little figure of a child with wings holding a scythe on top of the clock on the left suggest that the time for play is almost over and the children are about to enter the more dangerous grown-up world. Hogarth's favourite kind of painting was not portraits but stories of everyday life with a moral point to them. Here he has managed to combine the two.

Diagram to show chequerboard floor

William Hogarth 1697–1764
The Graham Children 1742
Oil on canvas, 161.9×181

Mares and Foals

Since it came to the Tate Gallery in 1959, this has been one of our most popular pictures and is recognised as a great masterpiece. But for a long time artists who painted animals or landscapes were regarded as inferior to those who painted gods, heroes or even just people. It was thought that a great painter should paint great subjects, so Stubbs did not get the fame his ability deserved. Now we believe that the way an artist paints is as important as what he paints.

Nevertheless horses were an important subject. They occupied a much more essential place in the world than they do today. They were the chief means of transport and of pulling farm machinery. They played an even more significant role among the landowners whose way of life centred on hunting and horse racing. Stubbs painted several pictures of mares and foals for great landowners, which hung in their houses with pictures of famous race winners and hunters. They show how much importance was attached to breeding horses just as the portraits of the family showed the importance of their own breeding.

Stubbs seems to want to let you see all the good points of the horses and therefore he has arranged them so that they do not overlap and hide one another. But, at the same time, he has painted each one in a different pose and from a different angle in order to show off his skill, to create a more interesting picture and make it look more natural. The horses seem to be looking at one another and form a group like people talking together. There is a beautiful landscape but Stubbs has kept it mostly low down and without strong colours so that it does not distract attention from the horses.

However, the most extraordinary thing about Stubbs' paintings of animals, especially when they are compared with those of any other artist of his day or before, is how much better he understood their bodies and the way they move. He had taught himself this by dissecting dead horses and drew the illustrations for a book of the anatomy of the horse. Stubbs is an example of an artist whose way of working was very close to that of a scientist: he based his pictures on a great deal of research.

George Stubbs 1724–1806
Mares and Foals in a Landscape 1760–70
Oil on canvas, 101.6 x 161.9

opposite page
An illustration drawn by Stubbs for the
book *The Anatomy of the Horse*

Giovanna Baccelli

This is a portrait of a famous Italian ballerina. Her name is pronounced roughly 'JoVARna BaCHELly'. She is wearing thick stage make-up and dancing in the costume she wore in a ballet called *Les Amants Surpris* (The lovers taken by surprise) which she performed in the season 1781–2. She had been born in Venice but lived in London where she was very well-known not only for her dancing but for her great charm and kindness.

Her lover, the Duke of Dorset, paid for this portrait but Baccelli probably chose the artist because Gainsborough was very musical and had many friends in the world of the theatre. The way he painted was very well suited to portraits of people in the theatre. He was particularly good at catching the effects of beauty, vivacity and charm. Above all, he was very skilful in showing the different qualities of fine materials, silks, satins, gauzes or velvets, and the effects of light shining on or through them. He did this by putting the paint on the canvas in many different ways: thick and thin, opaque and transparent, in fine brush strokes and big rough ones.

The small illustration, top, shows a part of the portrait enlarged. It does not look like anything much except squiggles of paint but, seen from a distance and with the rest of the dress around it, it falls into place. Compare it with the other detail, which is from the picture on the next page by Copley that was painted almost at the same time and is also part of a dress. This is much more carefully painted and the brush strokes are smoothed out, but the Gainsborough seems truer and more lively.

Unlike the picture by Copley, the Gainsborough has a background which is hardly there at all. Some fluffy paint just suggests the ground and some trees. You cannot tell whether they are real or part of the stage set. Artists generally only concentrate on what is necessary for the picture. The background is necessary for Copley because it is important that his battle took place in a particular town but Gainsborough is painting a person and it does not matter very much where she is.

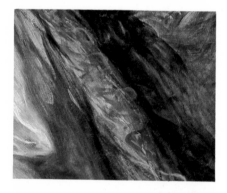

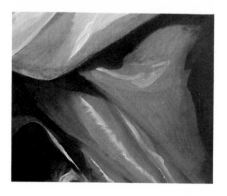

Thomas Gainsborough 1727–88
Giovanna Baccelli 1782
Oil on canvas, 226.7 x 148.6

opposite page top
Detail from 'Giovanna Baccelli'
opposite page bottom
Detail from 'The Death of Major
Peirson' by J. S. Copley

The Death of Major Peirson

On 5 January 1781, a force of 900 French soldiers attacked the island of Jersey in the Channel Islands and took the capital, St Helier. The British Governor was taken prisoner and ordered his troops to surrender. However, a young officer, Major Peirson, ignored the order, took command, counter-attacked and defeated the French. He was killed in the battle and then immediately revenged by his black servant. This is the story that is told in Copley's painting. You see Major Peirson dying in the arms of the other officers in the centre of the picture while the French officer who shot him is dying in the background to the right of the main group.

Copley was one of the painters who revived the art of painting the heroic events of his own time and his pictures had very much the effect of the modern films and television programmes that deal with that sort of subject. Many details of this picture were carefully researched and accurately painted. For example the buildings in the background can still be seen in St Helier, the uniforms both of British and French soldiers are correct and the officers were painted from life. But, just as in a television programme, even a documentary, some things are invented and included for effect. For example, the group on the right, who stand for the people of St Helier, are Copley's own family who lived in London. It is also most unlikely that the officers were all standing in a group away from their troops, and Copley has taken some liberties with time. The black servant seems to be in the act of firing his musket to avenge his master and yet the French soldier has already collapsed and is being supported by his companions.

The reason for this is that paintings, unlike films, cannot present events one after the other. Everything must be shown at the same time. Perhaps Copley is relying on the fact that the death of Peirson and the firing of the musket are large and will be seen at once, while you have to look for the dying Frenchman in the background and may see it a little later.

The way the story is told also shows what the painter and his audience would have found most important. The officers are very large but the ordinary soldiers and people of the island are pushed away to the edges and the French are very much in the background. Similarly, the officers are the actual individuals who took part while the soldiers are just types. No doubt the reason for this is that many of the people who went to art exhibitions and could afford to buy pictures were of the kind that provided the officers of the army and navy.

John Singleton Copley 1737–1815
The Death of Major Peirson, 6 January 1781 1783
Oil on canvas, 251.5 x 365.8

right
Details show the black servant
revenging the death of his master
and the dying French officer he
has shot

Elohim creating Adam

Blake was a great painter and a great poet. His poems and his paintings express the same poetic ideas about the world and its people but both may be difficult to understand.

Elohim is one of the names used in the Bible for God the Father and so this picture shows the story of the creation of the first man. But Blake is not just illustrating a very well-known story which hundreds of artists have painted. He gives it his own special meaning. For him the creation was not a happy event because he believed that all men are created to be trapped in a world of objects which repress their imagination. The symbol of this repression in the picture is the huge worm, which is wrapping itself around Adam's leg and body. Adam seems to be in agony and Elohim is very grim. Behind them is the sphere of the world and around it the storm of chaos into which the world came.

Blake believed that thought and imagination do not come from seeing, hearing or touching things in the world but directly from the soul. There is therefore almost nothing natural or realistic about the way he represents his subjects. He often borrowed images from other artists because for him artists were a special kind of people who could see the truth behind the appearance of things.

The lines in this work are very strong and are the main element of the design. Blake does not make any difference, as Gainsborough had done, between things that are solid and things that are soft. Hair, feathers and cloth all seem to be made of the same material. The long lines and the wide gestures of the figures give a very powerful feeling of energy to the painting and it is this sense of energy that is the most striking thing about his style.

This is the first time I have used the word 'style' in this book. It means the special character that appears in all the work of an artist and is as much a part of the way a painting affects you as the subject of it. The differences I have described between the painter of the 'Cholmondeley Sisters' and Hogarth or between Gainsborough and Copley are differences of style. It includes both the particular way the paint is put on which is like your handwriting and is so unique to you that an expert can distinguish it from anyone else's way (see p.71), and the way you arrange the parts of the picture.

Engraved figure by R. Dalton from the book *Antiquities and Views in Greece and Egypt*

William Blake 1757–1827
Elohim creating Adam 1795
Colourprint and watercolour,
43.2 x 53.7

Flatford Mill

Constable is perhaps England's best-loved painter. His pictures of the English countryside now seem so natural and typical that it is hard to believe that he had to struggle for years to be accepted. He painted a number of portraits but was mainly a specialist in landscape. I have already mentioned that this was not regarded as one of the highest forms of art. Among the ways in which artists had tried to raise the status of landscape painting was to put into them figures from bible stories or the gods and heroes of ancient Greece and Rome. Constable would not do this and it was one reason why he had to wait so long.

The picture we now call 'Flatford Mill' was originally named by him 'Scene on a Navigable River' and this shows that he intended it as a typical scene of the countryside at work, not as the portrait of a particular place nor simply as a beautiful view. It is inhabited by the people, including young boys, who worked on the farms and river mills. Constable's family owned Flatford Mill. The barge moving up river on the left may be one of their barges on its way to another family mill at Dedham and it may also have been built in the boatyard owned by the family. They were even responsible for the maintenance of the lock gates. Constable had worked for a short time in the business before turning to painting and was very familiar with every aspect of the land as the working place of the producers of food and other necessities.

Most of his pictures are of the countryside in which he had lived and it was full of personal associations. They are also based on a careful study of what he saw – not only the trees, fields, river-banks and man-made objects in the countryside but of the way they are affected by human use and by wind, erosion and all natural forces. He studied the different qualities of light at various times of the year and day, in different weather conditions and on different surfaces: water, earth, leaves and grass. He did not just put down what he looked at but always worked hard to bring everything together to make a painting which would sum up and give the total effect of what he had seen. Each large picture is based on a number of drawings and sketches in which he recorded details of what he wanted to include and tried out the effects that he aimed at.

John Constable 1776–1837
Flatford Mill (Scene on a Navigable River) 1817
Oil on canvas, 101.6 x 127

opposite page
A study of trees by Constable, 1817

Snow Storm

Today, Turner is probably regarded as England's greatest artist and in his own day had a very high reputation, but even he was strongly criticised. The picture opposite was condemned as 'soapsuds and whitewash' and Turner himself said 'no one had any business to like it'. But this did not mean that he thought it was not a *good* picture, he meant that it was not a *pleasant* one.

It is the record of a particular experience. The full title is 'Snow Storm – Steam Boat off a Harbour's Mouth making Signals in Shallow Water and going by the lead. The Author was in this storm on the night the Ariel left Harwich'. In such conditions, shallow water is specially dangerous and the fact that the ship's captain is having to measure the depth by dropping a piece of lead on a cord into the sea in order to find his way, shows how desperate the position was.

Turner said later 'I wanted to show what such a scene was like. I got the sailors to lash me to the mast to observe it; I was lashed for four hours and I did not expect to escape; but I felt bound to record it if I did'. Turner, like Constable, has not painted simply what he saw at any particular moment – probably with the wild movement of the boat, the noise and the air full of snow and spray, he could not have fixed anything in his mind. The picture shows *what it was like* to be there recreated later in his studio: the effect of the overpowering force of the wind and the sea, caught up together in a swirl of pure energy around the fragile little ship. She is a paddle steamer, her mast is bent by the storm and the smoke from her funnel is whipped away to join the gale. It is as if the gale had also taken charge of the paint which rushes together and round the canvas to evoke the surge of the waves and streaming snowflakes.

Turner was right to say no one had any business to like it but one can feel the fear, excitement and sense of being almost helpless at the mercy of nature that he had on that day. To stimulate feelings like these are just as much the work of an artist as to offer conventional pleasure or beauty. You can learn from them to respond in new ways to what goes on around you and respond with a new kind of pleasure to what may have seemed before just dangerous or ugly.

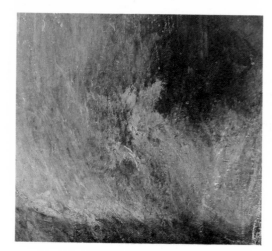

Detail to show the movement created by Turner's brush strokes

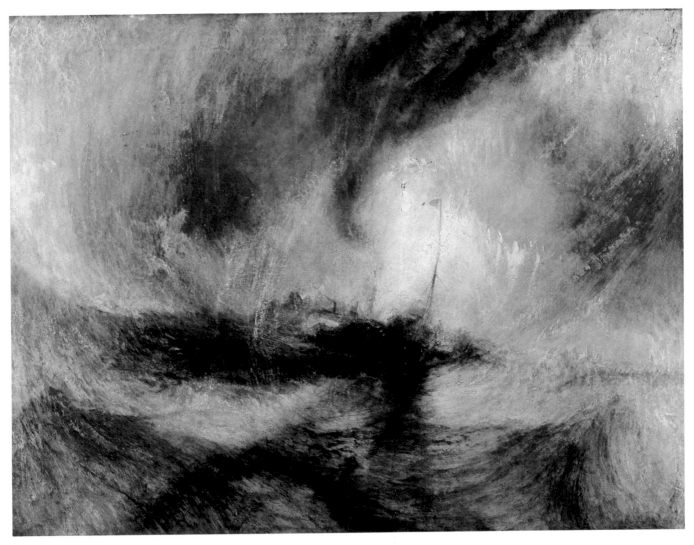

J. M. W. Turner 1775–1851
Snow Storm: Steam-boat off a Harbour's Mouth 1842
Oil on canvas, 91.4 x 121.9

The Carpenter's Shop

When this painting was first exhibited, Dickens wrote about it: 'Prepare yourselves for the lowest depths of what is mean, odious, repulsive and revolting'. Obviously he did not like the picture, but there is some justice in his comment. Millais wanted to show a different kind of truth to the one assumed by those painters who had tried to suggest the goodness of the members of the Holy Family by making them look unnaturally beautiful and noble. Millais' truth is that they were particular human beings and that he could make this plain by using ordinary people as models, painting them very exactly in every detail.

He set out to collect material for his picture in order to make it authentic. Every part was painted from a real object. The carpenter's shop was an actual one, then in Oxford Street, London, and the tools are those of his own day. The body of St Joseph was drawn from a carpenter so that the muscles would be developed correctly.

If you compare the painting with the drawing you can see Millais working out how to make his picture more true to life. The heads of the two older people in the drawing are just types which he has imagined while in the picture they are very much individuals, actually his own parents. He has also made the human relationship between the figures more natural. Both in the drawing and in the painting Jesus has cut his hand in the place where he would be nailed to the cross about thirty years later. In the drawing he kisses his mother as if to comfort her because she seems to realise this is going to happen. In the picture she turns to kiss him which is a more ordinary thing to do. The woman on the right folding a sheet has been replaced by St John bringing a bowl of water to wash the cut and Mary is no longer trying to do her embroidery in a carpenter's dirty workshop.

In spite of all these natural details the meaning of the picture depends on symbols. That is things which stand for events, ideas or people that were not actually part of the scene. For example, the sheep stand for the members of the Christian Church and the dove for the Holy Spirit. The ladder and pincers stand for those that were used to take Christ off the cross after his crucifixion. Most of all, the point of the story is that things happened to Jesus when he was young which foretold what would happen to him as a man – like the wound in his hand.

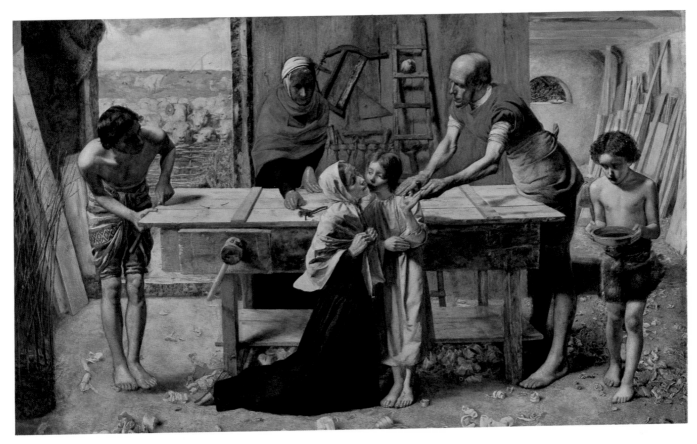

Sir John Everett Millais 1828–96
Christ in the House of His Parents
(The Carpenter's Shop) 1850
Oil on canvas, 86.4 x 139.7

right
Study for 'Christ in the House of His Parents' *c.*1849
Drawing and watercolour, 19.1 x 33.7

Fairy Feller's Master Stroke

If you look closely at the original of this quite small painting you can find more than fifty fairies and elves among the grass stems, flowers, leaves and seeds. In a long poem, written about the time he finished it, the painter tells us that they have gathered at the command of the white bearded man in the middle with a gold hat and club. They are watching the Fairy Feller in brown who is about to split open a nut with his axe to make a new carriage for the Fairy Queen Mab. Her tiny figure can be seen riding in the old one across the brim of the bearded man's hat. This idea comes from Shakespeare's *Romeo and Juliet*, 'Queen Mab . . . comes . . . drawn with a team of little atomies . . . her wagoner a small, grey coated gnat . . . Her chariot is an empty hazel nut.'

Dadd describes all the figures. At the top is a group including Tinker, Tailor, Soldier, Sailor from the nursery rhyme and below them, with crowns, Oberon and Titania from *A Midsummer Night's Dream.* Most of the rest are Dadd's own invention. Dadd's poem tells you that you can believe the picture or not and you can give it any meaning you like. His own business is only to make it all as real and as exact as he can. Fantasies are much more effective in painting when they seem very real. Compare with the Dali on page 39.

We also learn from his poem that he began just with a canvas on which he spread some paint roughly. He looked at this in the way that you look at clouds and painted what the marks seemed to suggest. This allowed his fantasy to grow far beyond the original idea. Perhaps it is also why the whole picture seems full from bottom to top. It was an unusual way of working.

The long thin grasses are a beautiful invention. They partly hide the fairies and make you believe that you might have missed them even though they were there all the time. They also show you what size the figures are – it would be difficult to tell otherwise.

It is a very skilfully painted picture and rather funny, but during the long time Dadd was painting it he was in a lunatic asylum where he had been sent for killing his father. He was shut up for forty-five years. Although it is rather strange, I do not think that the picture was obviously painted by someone who was insane or had done something so horrible. It is often difficult to see how the life and painting of artists are connected, even in this extraordinary case.

Richard Dadd 1817–86
**The Fairy Feller's Master
Stroke** 1855–64
Oil on canvas, 54 x 39.4

opposite page
Detail of Queen Mab riding in
her carriage across the brim of
the bearded man's hat

A Favourite Custom

During the late nineteenth century and early twentieth, painters and sculptors came to be divided into two groups which can be described as 'Avant Garde', from a military term meaning the leading group, and 'Academic'. Most of the remaining works described in this book belong to the Avant Garde and are also called 'Modern Art'. The reason why I will concentrate on 'Modern Art' is that most of the new ideas have appeared in the work of avant-garde artists or at least they can be seen there in their simplest and most extreme form. But Academic Art still flourishes and is exhibited, among many other places, at the Royal Academy from which it takes the name given to it in this country. As you will see there are many kinds of modern art but there are equally many kinds of academic art and of course there are also many artists, like Spencer, (p.37), who cannot be easily considered in either group.

The word 'academy' also means a school or college and one aspect of academic art is that it often seeks to preserve and use the skills handed down and taught by earlier generations of artists. The Royal Academy had a school from the beginning, where some of the great and successful artists taught the students. The teaching followed a particular tradition that began with the Greeks and Romans and was revived or invented anew and greatly extended in the Renaissance about 500 years ago. It gave a high value to representing people and things in a carefully constructed illusion of space (see p.64) and also to certain subjects, above all the great events of religion, history and myth. The most important aspect of art teaching was drawing the naked human body because people were the means by which almost everything was expressed.

'A Favourite Custom' shows what had happened to that tradition by the beginning of the twentieth century. There are nude figures and others carefully arranged in a variety of different poses, all in a well drawn space. The subject matter is Roman and the artist has done some research to get the clothes and furniture right. He has also studied the materials he wants to show us, particularly the graining of marble. In fact a great deal of thought and skill has gone into the picture.

But what is the real subject of the 'Favourite Custom'? Well it is people splashing each other in the swimming pool – nothing heroic or ancient but something that happened every day in the public baths that were appearing everywhere at the time the picture was painted. It is a modern subject in an ancient setting, painted to make you smile.

Sir Lawrence Alma-Tadema
1836–1912
A Favourite Custom 1909
Oil on wood, 66 × 45.1

The Pool of London

Cargo ships unloading were an ordinary kind of sight in Derain's day and he wanted to be sure that French people looking at it would know this was London, so he has put the famous Tower Bridge right in the middle near the top.

On the other hand, the way in which this picture was painted was a great shock to people at the time. Derain and his friends were called the wild beasts, *Les Fauves*. The name has stuck but the picture now looks cheerful rather than dangerously wild. This is an example of how pictures look different to people of different periods.

The most obvious things about the picture are that it is painted in very strong, bright colours and that these are put on with long or short brush strokes which are not smoothed over. Each patch is more or less the same colour all over and the colours are separate from each other.

The effect of this is that the artist seems to be painting very directly, getting his colours straight out of the tube and putting them down without having to make alterations and without changing his mind. This is why it seems so straightforward. But the colours are not just any colours. They are mostly what are called the primary colours – red, yellow and blue, together with their opposites; green for red, violet for yellow and orange for blue. A book had been published by a scientist called Chevreul which was read by many artists. In it he showed that, if colours which are opposites are placed close together, the difference between them looks stronger. In this picture you can see that if Derain wants to make something stand out strongly he puts green and red together or blue with orange or yellow, but when he wants to make them to stand out less, like Tower Bridge in the slightly misty distance, he uses two colours which are close, a blue green and a yellowish green. In some places you can see him painting just the effect which Chevreul had described. Where the main mast of the ship is seen against the green sky it becomes much redder.

All the same, the picture is not painted according to a theory – some of the colours are just stronger versions of the natural colours he would have seen or that were at least probable. It is rather like when we are talking and joking happily and we exaggerate everything we say. It is unusual to find pictures painted in this spirit, no wonder it was a surprise at the time but now we can enjoy it easily.

André Derain 1880–1954 (French)
The Pool of London 1906
Oil on canvas, 65.7×99

opposite page
Photograph of the Pool of London in the
early twentieth century. Reproduced by
kind permission of the Museum of London

Seated Nude

Just as Derain and his group were called the 'Fauves' in 1905, Picasso and his friends were called 'Cubists'. Although not exactly cubes, the straight lines and angles of 'Seated Nude' show why they got this name but, unlike Derain's picture, this one remains rather difficult to understand even now, seventy years later.

One reason for this is that while Derain painted more or less the shapes he saw but gave them his own vivid colours Picasso has changed the shapes so the objects are more difficult to identify. In addition, Picasso has treated the figure in the same way as its surroundings so that it does not stand out. If you look carefully you can pick out a woman with her right arm bent across her body under her breasts and the left down with a hand on her right leg. She is sitting on a chair which has round-topped arms that come forward on either side below her elbows and a high, square back. A curtain or piece of material falls over one corner of this at the top left. Although all this is hard to see, Picasso tried to help by choosing a subject which was very commonplace at the time so that viewers would have something to start from.

Bright colours have been left out because the picture is mainly concerned with shape. The problem for the painter is that the shape of most objects changes as you move round them, but if you show an object from only one position you do not tell everything you can about it. Engineering draughtsmen, for example, often do three different drawings of the same object so that craftsmen can understand the shapes completely enough to make a real object from them.

In this picture Picasso has several different view points but they are brought together into one flat image. A human body has two each of many parts so he can show one from one view point and the other from another. The woman's right shoulder (on the left of the picture) is seen from above and rather outside the body, so that it shows the connection of the shoulder joint with the shoulder blade, while the second is seen from below and across the body so that it shows the angle between the ball of the joint and the pit behind the collar bone. Generally surfaces facing upwards are painted sandy colours and those facing downwards, greyish. The hard lines indicate the edges of each part that is seen from one view point. But the effect of these is to divide up the figure into facets like a diamond which is what gives these pictures the look that led to them being called 'cubist'.

Although the main purpose of the painting was to make a kind of experiment in the way in which shapes can be represented there is no doubt that Picasso understood that the effect of this would be to take the body to pieces and would be seen as a violent distortion of a human being.

Pablo Picasso 1881–1973
(Spanish, lived in France)
Seated Nude 1909–10
Oil on canvas, 92.1 x 73

below
Diagram to show seated figure

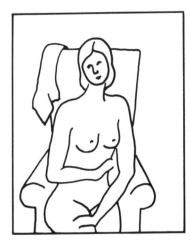

Cossacks

Although I have not used the word abstract, the way I have described the last two pictures has shown that they were at the beginning of what is called abstract art. In language, an ordinary noun stands for a thing or type of thing in the world but an abstract noun stands for a quality that all sorts of objects may have: brightness or roundness. In rather the same way, even though one was a river scene and the other a person, Derain's picture mainly deals with the quality of brightness of colour and Picasso's with the quality of shape.

Kandinsky's picture is still more abstract. If you have not seen what it represents you can begin to read it when you look again at the title and the artist's name – a Russian name. It is a battle in old Russia. On the right are three Cossack soldiers in white cloaks with red hats and yellow beards. Two have long lances but the one on the left stretches out his arm and holds a sword with its point to the ground. Behind them is a blue hillside and on it a castle. Above this a flock of birds is flying. In the middle is a rainbow – the easiest thing to recognise – and above, much too large for their place in the picture, two men fighting on horseback. These are more difficult to work out. The red hair or hat of one is at the top middle with a large pink sabre raised to strike, the black curve just below is his other arm; and then there is the horse, also represented by black lines, its head a rectangle with a sort of smile to the left of the man. Below this is the sabre of the other soldier who also has a red hat and apparently a green beard or collar. The jumble of curved lines and angles between the horses is their front legs tangled together as they rear up against one another.

Although it is possible to work out what almost every part of this picture refers to in this way, it is not really necessary. If Kandinsky had wanted to show the details of the uniforms, the expressions on the faces or just where everything was in the landscape, he would have done so. What he was after is more difficult to explain. He had in mind the power of music to affect people by means of tunes, rhythms and harmonies that may sometimes recall natural sounds and feelings but do not depend on an exact imitation of these. In the same way he composed his picture of colours, smooth and jagged shapes, straight and curved lines which recall the parts of his subject, the battle, but do not imitate it. The mood, just as in a musical composition changes from one part to another, calm and blue on the lower right, quick and active above.

Wassily Kandinsky 1866–1944
(Russian, worked in Russia, Germany and France)
Cossacks 1910–11
Oil on canvas, 94.6 x 145.4

Grey, Red, Yellow and Blue

The pictures by Picasso and Kandinsky are abstract but, as I have shown, natural shapes can be seen in them even though they are simplified and altered. In the painting opposite there are no natural shapes. The picture is completely abstract and does not represent anything.

It is made up entirely of elements which are drawn from the art of painting. The most important is the canvas itself which is divided into a grid. The grid is made up of vertical and horizontal lines that are parallel to the sides of the canvas. The areas between the lines are filled in with areas of the three primary colours (p.66) red, yellow and blue and with a range of tones or values from dark to light: black, dark grey, light grey. The effect of the picture depends first on the simplicity of these elements, then on the fact that they correspond to something very basic in the way people think and describe things. There are three categories we use all the time – *opposites*: 'good' and 'bad', 'male' and 'female' (in the picture the opposites are vertical and horizontal), *ranges*: 'big', 'bigger', 'biggest', (in the picture light grey, dark grey and black) and *individual qualities* (red, yellow and blue).

The way we use these words and categories allows us to fit everything in the universe into them: everything can be said to be either 'good' or 'bad', has a size from very small to very large, etc. So that quite a small number of categories can cover an enormous variety of things. Mondrian's picture uses a small number of categories to stand for everything that can be in a picture. The other and perhaps even more important part of the effect of the picture is due to the proportions of the rectangles and the arrangement of them. The coloured rectangles are placed carefully in different parts of the picture so that each colour and tone appears next to each of the others. The colours are mixed with pale grey so that the difference between them is less sharp. The proportions of the rectangles are carefully varied between very tall and very wide. The only large squares are divided so they do not stand out. There is one at the top right hand corner divided into pale grey, black and blue and one near the middle which is yellow and red. The canvas itself is square. It is divided by every line but only one is allowed to run completely across the picture; all the others are incomplete so all the parts hold together.

Overall, the intention seems to be to create the maximum variety and harmony out of the simple rules the artist has given himself so the picture stands for the idea that the essence of nature, which presents to us its own infinite variety and harmony, can be represented very simply.

opposite page
Piet Mondrian 1872–1944
(Dutch, worked in Holland, France, England and America)
Composition with Grey, Red, Yellow and Blue 1920–27
Oil on canvas, 99.7 x 100.3

Maternity

Although most of the objects in the collection of the Tate Gallery are paintings, prints and drawings which are on flat surfaces, the Tate also has a collection of sculpture: objects which have another dimension, depth as well as height and width. Pictures, as I have shown, often try to give an illusion of this third dimension, but sculptures exist in our own real space, like the furniture in our rooms. The art of the sculptor is in making real objects and for this reason sculptors have been particularly interested in the materials they use. These materials affect the look of the sculpture and what the artist can do.

There are three main ways of making a sculpture: *assembling* – fixing it together out of pieces, *carving* – cutting away from a block until the shape is reached and *modelling* – working a soft material like clay or plasticine until it takes on the shape you want. I have chosen three sculptures which show what can be done with each of these (see pp.41 and 49).

'Maternity' is assembled. The artist had been trained as an iron worker and welder and the sculpture is welded together out of iron rods, tubes, rings and discs. They are like the lines of a drawing which sketch in the shapes but do not fill them out solidly. The method of welding iron rods allows the artist to construct lines in the three dimensions of space.

The subject is a mother and child, that is why it is called 'Maternity'. The artist only puts in enough recognisable bits of a person for you to be able to work out what it is. At the top you see two eyes and long hair streaming out to the right and left, below are two breasts, indicated by a disc with a nail through it and a ring. The baby is three bits of bar and a thin rod bent into a right angle, just below these. Below there is a sort of cone of rods for the skirt. The thicker right angled piece does not look like the legs but may stand for their function of holding the figure up.

The artist does not wish to show a complete figure but the use of rods allows him first to suggest it and then to do something else. What he has done I think is to create an image of anxiety or fear. The woman is not at all maternal, not soft, rounded or solid. Her breast is a spike. The rods suggest tension and the hair streams out like the hair of a person running away or blown by a strong wind. The baby too is angular and spiky. The sculpture on page 41 shows a very different kind of mother.

opposite page
Julio Gonzalez 1876–1942
(Spanish, worked in Spain and France)
Maternity 1934
Metal sculpture, 130.5 x 40.6 x 23.5

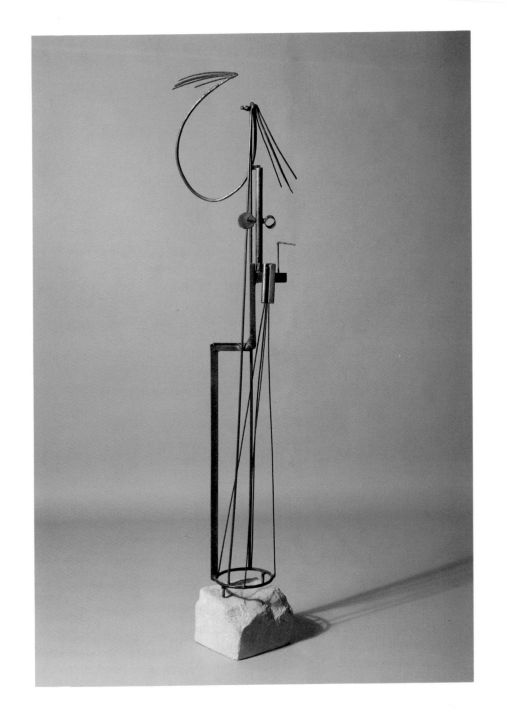

St Francis and the Birds

The subject of this painting is the Italian saint, Francis of Assisi, who felt so much love for every creature in the world that he could talk to them. He gave a sermon to a flock of birds. But, like almost all of Spencer's paintings, the story is set in Cookham, the village where he lived. You can see an English tiled cottage and the birds of an English farmyard: chickens, ducks and pigeons.

Spencer had just painted a memorial chapel to men who were killed in the 1914–18 war and he wanted to do a chapel about peace. This was not to be an actual building but the village of Cookham itself. The main street was to be the nave, the river was to be an aisle and he would fill them with pictures. The figures of the saints would be the local people. His St Francis was his father who once had his trousers stolen and went about in a dressing gown that looked like the saint's brown robe. Spencer remembered seeing his father in the lane between 'Fernlea', which was the Spencer's cottage, and 'The Nest' next door, the ivy-covered cottage on the right of the picture. He was getting food for the hens and ducks from the larder and they were following him. So the picture records a particular occasion which resembled the subject of the picture, St Francis and the birds.

Spencer explained that St Francis is large and spread out to show that his teaching spread far and wide. In the picture he does not so much speak to the birds as speak upwards to God for them. It is not explained why St Francis and the boy beyond him in a blue jersey have their hands on the wrong way round unless it is to suggest they are turned both to God and the birds.

Spencer was standing up for an artist's right to have his say and to do what he thinks proper even though other people may not like it. The fact that he paints people and things that can easily be recognised, only makes the oddness of them more obvious.

In our society artists are generally thought to be very unusual people. This allows them a great deal of freedom in what they do and how they live but it makes it easy for others to think that what artists do does not concern ordinary people. This book tries to show that is not true.

Giotto, **St Francis** c. 1300

Sir Stanley Spencer
1891–1959 (English)
St Francis and the Birds 1935
Oil on canvas, 66 x 58.4

Autumnal Cannibalism

Although many people think art should be beautiful and pleasing it has often dealt with ugliness, pain and horror. Some of the most successful films, for example, are full of fear and violence. In the early part of this century psychiatrists, especially Freud, tried to show how pleasure and pain, reason and unreason are linked together. One of their main techniques was the study of dreams. Artists like Dali (the Surrealists) have used these ideas to paint pictures.

Our century has been a very violent one and one in which horrifying events have been instantly brought to everyone's attention in newspapers, magazines, newsreels and television. 'Autumnal Cannibalism' was painted in the year of the beginning of the Spanish Civil War and the artist has said that it represents the Spanish people devouring each other. In the background on the right you see a Spanish landscape burned by the sun, on the left a desert or beach. In the foreground two revolting figures, which seem to be half-melted humans, are eating each other. One of them reaches right round the other and accidentally cuts into its own body. This one, on the left, with its paler skin and blouse open at the front is a woman the other a man. They are on a chest of drawers which is empty, or perhaps this is the lower part of their bodies joined together. This chest of drawers, like the crutches and ants which also appear in many of Dali's pictures, is like the obsession described by psychiatrists – an image which comes to you again and again and will not go away.

There are no obvious indications of war – no planes, guns or soldiers. If the picture represents the war, it represents it in the way that nightmares often do – the sense of horror and fear is very powerful but the events are strange and distorted. The feelings have been transferred to another, and private, set of images. Freud had shown that dreams work in the same sort of way. I cannot give you an exact meaning for everything in the picture. If I could, perhaps its power would be weakened, like magic. All the same, it seems that the idea of the Spaniards living together in one country, dependent on one another but unable to stop attacking and trying to dominate one another, is mixed by Dali with an image of the love between a man and a woman which can be very hurtful. Dali shows that the relationship is mindless and blind by painting figures without faces, particularly without eyes. They have no bones so they cannot move and help themselves.

The picture is painted like the 'Fairy Feller' (p.23) with great clarity and detail so that it seems to have the overwhelming reality of a nightmare from which you cannot escape.

opposite page
Salvador Dali b.1904
(Spanish, worked mainly in Spain and America)
Autumnal Cannibalism 1936
Oil on canvas, 65.1 x 65.1

Recumbent Figure

When he carved this figure, Henry Moore was particularly concerned with bringing out the qualities of the materials he was using and with adapting his sculpture to them.

He first deliberately chose a stone that was quarried in his own country. It has a strong, gritty texture and is a very stony sort of stone. The figure is extremely bulky and emphasises the heaviness of stone. The rounded shapes are like those of natural rocks weathered by the sea. Moore leaves as much as he can of the original block that he carved so that you can see what shape it was before he began to work. There is another way in which he asserts that the sculpture is carved in stone. Although the figure can be recognised as a woman it has a hole right through its chest. If you made a hole in the body of a person you would find bones and innards. Moore's hole reveals, of course, only more stone.

All of this is not just a private game that the artist is playing. He is using it to suggest a very old and important idea. This is that a woman, your mother, was the place in which you grew from a seed and that she fed and supported you when you were a child. She is therefore like the earth itself. Many people have worshipped a goddess as earth-mother. Moore shows an earth-mother by representing her as a rock, making her seem as stable and permanent as possible. She does not have a face, to show changing expression, or hands, to give and take, or legs to walk away. She is basically a body on which life grows.

The outline of the figure is also like the hills and rocks of a landscape. Moore has been able to give his figure extra meaning – just as Nash was to do in 'Totes Meer' (p.43) by making his image represent two things at the same time.

The theme of the recumbent or reclining woman has been one to which Moore has returned again and again. The small pictures show some others which were modelled and which are quite different – not so massive and rounded. But they still make the same statement that a woman is like the land.

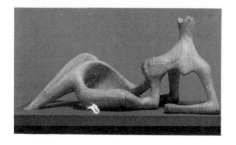

Henry Moore b.1898 (English)
Recumbent Figure 1938
Stone sculpture, 89 x 132.7 x 73.7

opposite page top
Reclining Figure (Lincoln Center) 1963–5, bronze
opposite page bottom
Reclining Figure 1951, plaster

Totes Meer

The title is in German and means 'Dead Sea'. This painting, like the sculpture by Moore, is one in which the image seems to represent two things at the same time or perhaps it represents a change taking place. One thing is turning into another so that what you feel about one is transferred to the other.

It shows first of all a dump where the bits of German bombers and fighters that were shot down in the Battle of Britain were collected. At the same time you seem to see waves breaking on a beach. The greenish grey of the Dorniers, Heinkels and Messerschmidts tosses and curls like breaking rollers and a pale shadow lies on the yellow earth like the thin water left on a sandy beach by the receding waves. The moon above strengthens the feeling of death and defeat.

The image was a good one because the German planes came over in waves at night and many were shot down or turned back over the south coast; when the moon shone it was easier to find them and attack. The main part of the picture was taken quite directly from a photograph. But the truth of the painting is beyond this.

It is quite rare in modern times for an artist in the West to work for his or her country but Nash worked twice as a war artist; in the 1914–18 war and in the 1939–45 war. On each occasion he produced images which seemed to fit exactly both the facts and the mood of the people at war. Each time, although he was an official artist in a patriotic war, he produced paintings which show as much compassion for the enemy as for his own side.

We are all relieved when the waves beat on the shore and do not sweep over it and the British were naturally thankful when the raids were turned back and people were neither killed by the bombs nor their houses destroyed. But the picture by Nash is full of sadness which includes pity for the German airmen who were killed and wounded in their machines. The picture does not seem to gloat or boast. It remains therefore a powerful image even though the battle was over more than thirty-five years ago.

Photograph by Paul Nash of wrecked aircraft, Cowley Dump, 1940
Tate Gallery Archives

Paul Nash 1889–1946 (English)
Totes Meer 1940–1
Oil on canvas, 101.6 x 152.4

Industrial Landscape

Like Spencer, Lowry painted his own world. This was not the small, picturesque world of a Thames-side village but industrial Lancashire and its working people. Lowry's pictures seem to catch the mood of it so perfectly that everyone can recognise the scene. The mood, like the weather, is often bitter and depressing but this does not put you off – the people in the pictures seem to know how to live there.

The people are a bit like match-stick men with large feet. Although they seem to share the same life, they do not seem to talk to each other much and most of them are walking alone. In fact, although the scene is very real, it is not actually very naturalistic. For example, if you photograph people walking about, you catch them at every part of the stride but Lowry nearly always shows them at the point where one foot is forward and the other just lifting from the ground behind. This is his effective convention for people walking and is like the eighteenth-century convention for animals running described on page 69.

The painting is not a view of any particular place but it is full of typical buildings of northern towns, the terraced cottages of the workers, the mills and factories, water-towers and gasometers. Among them are the grander buildings put up by the local authorities and businessmen. There is one in the middle of the picture at the end of the street with a tall tower behind it and several domes in the distance.

One of the most important things about the old industrial towns is the wasted and derelict space between the roads and buildings where people gather. Lowry is very good at creating this space. You can see how he divides his picture up into three or four bands of buildings beginning with the row of cottages in the foreground and ending with the cream-coloured factory in the centre of the picture. These bands run right across from edge to edge and the people walk and gather in the gaps.

Beyond this the spaces become naturally more confused together. It is only a background. There are no people, tops of large buildings can be seen through the smoke and mist, above all the factory chimneys which dominate the scene. In the further distance the smoke hides every-thing in a whitish veil which reaches up to the clouds.

L. S. Lowry 1887–1976 (English)
Industrial Landscape 1955
Oil on canvas, 114.3 x 152.4

opposite page
Detail to show Lowry's 'match-stick men' figures

Light Red over Black

Very often the most interesting and the best pictures are those we can say a great deal about but, like music, some pictures bring out feelings that are so powerful and particular that we cannot find words to speak about them. For me, Rothko's picture has that effect.

Some of Rothko's pictures are brightly coloured and convey a feeling of excitement and happiness but this one, with its dark shapes blotting out a blood red background, appears sombre and tragic. Rothko is said to have felt that his pictures were successful when people wept tears as they looked at them. This has been the ambition of some writers and dramatists and of some artists who have painted pictures of tragic events, but Rothko does not need any images of people to make us feel such emotions, he does it directly with colours and shapes.

The picture should be looked at steadily and quite close to for a fairly long time to have its full effect. It is then large enough to fill your eyes. The size of an abstract picture is often more important than that of a naturalistic picture, or a photograph. For you can enlarge or reduce them to any size and they still represent the same people or objects. But an abstract picture does not refer to any other object it just is what it is.

Rothko's shapes are simple but not sharply defined. They lie in the centre of the picture and are the same on one side as the other; that is they are symmetrical. They do not overlap or seem to hang in front of one another, they just float in a red space. It is for this reason perhaps that they seem like feelings. Feelings are not situated in particular places like objects are. They fill your mind.

It is the symmetry that seems to ask you to stand still in front of the picture. Perhaps this is because a person who is looking directly at you, and asking you to look back, faces you and appears symmetrical but if they do not want you to pay attention they may turn to one side and so do not appear symmetrical.

You can easily see how important these simple facts are if you try to paint a picture or imagine one with Rothko's colours but pushed to one side, tilted, overlapping or with sharp and irregular shapes.

Mark Rothko 1903–70 (American)
Light Red over Black 1957
Oil on canvas, 232.7 x 152.7

Cyclops

The process of modelling, in which soft materials are built up and pressed into shape, produces works which are not permanent and can easily be damaged or dry up and crumble away. It has always been usual for artists to make a cast of the model in some permanent metal, most often bronze.

The usual process is that the sculpture is first made in clay around a metal skeleton called an armature. It is then covered with plaster in sections that can be taken off. These can be put together again to form a mould. The inside of this mould is painted with wax or varnish so that it does not stick and can be filled again with plaster. When this sets it is exactly the same shape as the clay original and can be kept in case the mould gets damaged. To make the object in bronze, wax is poured into the empty mould so as to form a thick coating all over the inside of it and then the rest is filled in with a core of material which can be removed later. The mould is taken off the wax and replaced with another which will not be damaged by heat. The whole thing is then put in an oven so that the wax runs out leaving a space between the mould and the core. Molten metal is poured into this space. When it cools and hardens the mould and core are taken away leaving metal which can be smoothed and then polished.

'Cyclops' is not altogether typical but it shows what can be done with the technique. Paolozzi (Pow LOT sy) began by pressing little objects, including bits of toys, machinery and door fittings, into a sheet of clay. Then he melted wax and poured it over the clay so that, when it had hardened and been picked off the clay, it formed a sheet covered with the marks of the little objects. He then built up the sculpture from these sheets of wax, softening them with a flame so that he could bend them and stick them together. Finally it was cast in bronze in the way described above.

The sculpture has taken the form of a crude figure which seems to be half-human half-machine, a sort of science-fiction robot. Its single eye is the cast of the wheel of a plastic toy and you can see door catches and all sorts of bits all over it. Paolozzi chose the name 'Cyclops' because that was the name of a half-human giant with one eye in a Greek myth. He was blinded by the hero. Parts of the figure are left incomplete and the heat of the flame has melted others so that the robot seems damaged and distressed. In fact it seems badly wounded so there is something about this crazy, rickety tower which makes you feel sorry for it.

Eduardo Paolozzi b.1924
(Scottish, works in England)
Cyclops 1957
Bronze sculpture, 111.1 x 30.5 x 20.3

above
Detail showing all the strange bits
and pieces cast in bronze

Hyena Stomp

If you compare this picture with two other abstract pictures in this book, the Rothko on page 47 and the Mondrian on page 33, you can see how different they are to one another even though they are alike in some ways. This one is large like the Rothko and precise like the Mondrian. Its design is much more complicated than the Rothko but, unlike either of these, it is worked out on a system which is absolutely logical and could be carried out by anyone once the artist has invented it. It therefore seems impersonal.

The system is as follows. The artist chose eleven ready-made colours and arranged them in an order which follows the colour of the spectrum: from reds and oranges, through yellow, green and blue, ending with violet. He put the first colour in a band along the right-hand edge, then, with a diagonal joint, the next across the bottom, the next up the left, across the top and then down the right alongside the first, and so on through all eleven. Then he began all over again with red, three times until he got to the middle.

Not only is the picture completely worked out in this way, but, by arranging the colours in an order which can be understood by anyone who knows the order of colours in the rainbow, Stella makes it possible for the system to be guessed at once by many of the people who look at it. There is nothing secret or uncertain about it.

But the effect is unexpected. Because there are eleven colours and not twelve, when each colour comes again it appears on the side before the one it appeared last time. You can most easily see this with the yellow which begins at the right, the next is at the top, the next on the left then at the bottom and again at the right. This sets up a kind of rhythmic progression. By beginning the first colour with a square end and following on with diagonal joints at all the others he makes it clear which is the beginning but this also means that the diagonal line of joints at the top right does not meet the others in the middle. It seems out of step. In fact this device is rather like the unexpected but powerfully moving rhythm that is called syncopation, and is common in jazz music. The title of the picture 'Hyena Stomp' is that of a famous piece of jazz music.

opposite page
Frank Stella b. 1936 (American)
Hyena Stomp 1962
Acrylic on canvas, 195.6 x 195.6

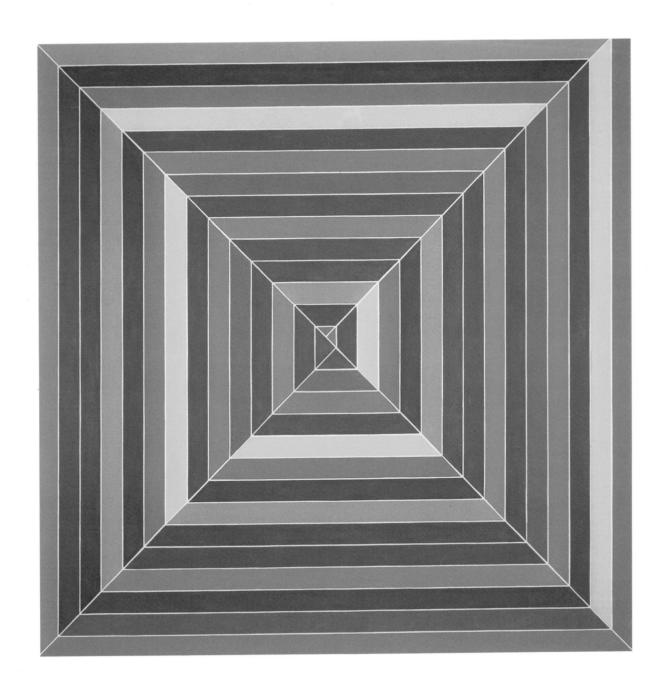

Whaam!

I have already described how art had divided between the avant-garde and academic about a hundred years ago. There has also been a division between fine art and popular art, such as posters, calendars and comics, similar to the division between classical and pop music. All the time, fine artists have used images taken from popular art just as popular or commercial artists have taken from fine art. But some artists in the 1950s and 1960s set out to do this, in a very direct way.

At first glance 'Whaam!' looks just like a frame from an American comic and was in fact taken from one of these comics. One reason for doing this was that Lichtenstein wanted to show that there was nothing that an artist could not turn into art and in the 1950s people who loved fine art generally agreed that there was nothing quite so debased as the American comics. The process by which Lichtenstein has turned the image into art is partly straightforward. Instead of being printed on cheap paper it is painted by hand on canvas. Instead of being a few inches square and part of a continuous story it is isolated and enlarged to the size of a large painting.

Although these changes may seem rather obvious and easy they do go along with something that painting has always done and continues to do. Artists take what is ordinary, make

Roy Lichtenstein b.1923 (American)
Whaam! 1963
Acrylic on canvas, 172.7 x 406.4

right
Preliminary drawing for 'Whaam!', 1963

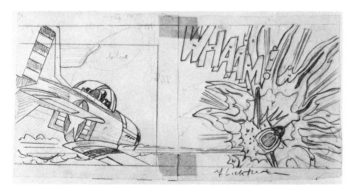

it of different materials and put it in a different context, in this case paint instead of printing, an art gallery instead of a comic book. By doing this, they draw attention to it and can make us look at it freshly and with new interest. But in fact Lichtenstein has not stopped at this point. He has changed the image in more subtle ways. He has divided it into two, partly as a joke, one canvas is shooting another down, and partly as a reference to an ancient kind of painting on two panels called a diptych. Often in diptychs the subject of one of the panels, a portrait, is looking at what is on the other.

The two canvases have different types of composition (see p.70). The one on the left, with its diagonals, is full of movement: from left to right and from the front into the distance. The other expands from a centre. It is almost as much like a flower as an explosion. Every shape, line or curve in both parts is worked on and refined. This is not so as to make the image more real, because the object which Lichtenstein is painting is not an aeroplane but a *picture* of an aeroplane. He is trying to make a more perfect picture of a less perfect one. All the changes I have described are aimed at transforming what was considered to be a debased image into one with the impact, clarity and organisation typical of a fine work of art.

Mr and Mrs Clark and Percy

Percy is the cat sitting on the lap of Ossie Clark, a famous fashion designer. His wife, Celia Birtwell, is a textile designer. Everything about the picture suggests the exquisite taste of the couple and their home: the subtle range of blue-green colours, the white cat, the lilies, the chair, the tiffany lamp standing by the telephone, the gilt framed print on the wall (by Hockney himself). There is a general air of neatness and of everything having been placed just so.

Hockney is a painter who is very sensitive to style – styles of painting, decorating, dressing and talking. His own ways of dressing and talking are unique and famous – he has become a star very much like the stars of pop music or films. But his painting is the most important part of a complete lifestyle which is very serious and a matter for much hard work, thought and judgment.

I began to show what style is when writing about the picture by William Blake on page 15. In fact all the descriptions in this book are in some way descriptions of styles but particularly those of the Picasso (p.29) and the Mondrian (p.33). Some artists like Picasso and Hockney change their style freely in order to get different effects. Hockney sometimes even deliberately imitates other artists' styles to make a special point. But a style may also be the way that an artist shows what kind of person he is himself and in this case it is very like the clothes we wear and the tones of voice that we use to express ourselves.

In our picture, Hockney has chosen a style which is at first glance very realistic. In fact it is based on lots of careful studies in pencil and chalks made of the Clarks in their own room and on photographs of details like the hands. But the effect of stylishness itself is something that Hockney shares with many of his subjects and has put into the picture. Like most of his portraits, this one is of intimate friends of his – people whom he constantly visits and whose way of life he affects as they affect his own. In order to bring out the sense of perfect taste, he used much art, simplifying and arranging shapes and surfaces, selecting the poses and relationships that are natural to the people, suggesting the subtle light of a London interior so that finally it is hard to see what is the style of the room and its inhabitants and what is the style of the artist.

David Hockney b. 1937 (English)
Mr and Mrs Clark and Percy 1970–1
Acrylic on canvas. 213.4 x 304.8

opposite page
Photograph of Ossie Clark taken
by Hockney – a study he used while
painting

A Hundred Mile Walk

This work of art seems quite different from any others in the book – you could not call it a painting, a sculpture or even entirely a drawing. It is a work of art made up of three elements of different kinds that work together to evoke a particular sense of the land we live in.

All the parts of the work relate to a particular walk taken by Long during a week over New Year 1971–2. On the left is a map on which he has drawn a circle which indicates the location and route of the walk, on the right is a photograph showing the kind of landscape which he passed through and seven phrases from among those that came into his head as he was walking, one for each day. These are not a complete description, they are merely indications which are just sufficient for you to make some kind of reconstruction in your imagination of Long's own feelings and experiences on this occasion, especially if you can read a map. You can get as much out of it as you put in.

For example, given the scale of the map, which is 1″ to the mile, you can work out that he walked round the same path about fourteen times to reach 100 miles – perhaps he went round twice a day, perhaps sometimes less, sometimes more. The photograph shows the way ahead as he walked. If you study the map and look for the course of a stream running along the route you can see that it was taken from the position of 10 on a clock dial and is looking north west towards the start. So he was walking round clockwise and about to complete a circle. If you follow the path now in your imagination, you can tell where he must have breathed hard, climbing a hill where the contours are close together and when he was on top of a peak with a wide view (2 on the clock).

For Richard Long, as for many artists, the interest is sometimes more in making the work of art, in their intentions, processes and feelings than in the finished object that the public can see. In fact all works of art can be thought of just as what the artist leaves when he has finished working.

All the same, most artists have worked primarily in order to create a finished object – a work of art. But Long, and many others in the last ten years, have deliberately produced works, which are carefully worked out and presented, but much of the interest comes from what you can deduce or imagine of the ideas and activity that lie behind them. The work may even be made rather unsatisfying or unexpected in a way that directs your attention to these things, to the thought and processes that made it rather than to itself.

Once you have made this imaginative exploration of the work you can go beyond it to what it reveals of the land itself and how we come to know it, not only by looking but by marking it out, through our bodies as we work in it or walk across it and by all the other senses.

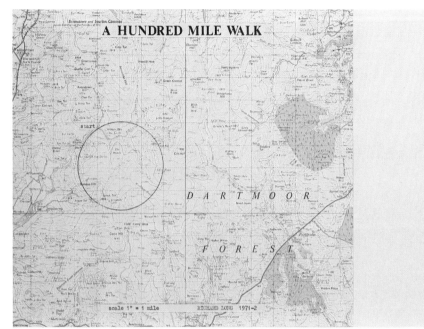

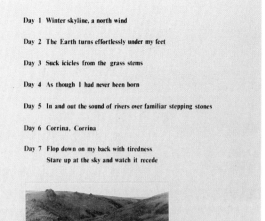

Day 1 Winter skyline, a north wind

Day 2 The Earth turns effortlessly under my feet

Day 3 Suck icicles from the grass stems

Day 4 As though I had never been born

Day 5 In and out the sound of rivers over familiar stepping stones

Day 6 Corrina, Corrina

Day 7 Flop down on my back with tiredness
       Stare up at the sky and watch it recede

Richard Long b.1945
A Hundred Mile Walk 1971–2
Mixed media

Media

This word refers to the materials that the artist uses and to their particular effects, qualities and limitations.

Drawing

At its simplest, this is a way of marking a surface – as with pencil or pen on paper. Drawing is basically a matter of lines and dots although you can make areas by putting lots of lines close together. It is often used by artists to note down the shape of things that they see or imagine and to distinguish light from dark. It can also be used to make a pattern or texture.

Thomas Girtin, **The White House, Chelsea** 1800

Drawings may be coloured with watercolour which is thin and soaks into the paper so that every mark the artist makes remains visible. Each new colour is affected by the colours underneath in a different way so that a skilful painter can get very subtle and complex results. This is one of the best ways to represent the effects of weather and of distance in landscape. The thicker kind of waterpaint, poster paint or powder paint often used by designers and in schools, is not transparent like the usual artist's watercolour. Each brush stroke more or less covers up what has gone before. It gives brighter, stronger colours and is also used by some artists. It is often referred to as gouache (goo-ARSH).

Oil paint

Traditionally the most important way of painting has been in oil paint on canvas or on wooden panels. This kind of paint is similar to that used on furniture or houses. It is made of tiny grains of coloured material mixed with a kind of oil which dries and hardens. Oil paint can be made thin so that it is transparent like watercolour or it can be thick enough to stand up from the surface of the picture like icing on a cake, as illustrated below. It may be shiny like gloss paint or matt like emulsion. More recently artists have used artificial paints based on materials similar to plastics: acrylic and vinyl, which can do all these things too.

Thomas Gainsborough, **Giovanna Baccelli** detail

John Constable, **Flatford Mill** detail

André Derain, **The Pool of London** detail

Salvador Dali, **Autumnal Cannibalism** detail

The paint is put on with a palette knife or most often with brushes, which range from soft, pointed ones that will make a dot or thin line of colour to ones that are as broad as house painters' brushes and make a big wide mark. Artists sometimes put the paint on in separate dabs or long strokes which they leave untouched. But they can also spread and smooth out the paint so that these marks do not show – compare the two details above. They have also used their fingers, rollers (like the ones you can use on walls) and sprays. Sometimes they scrape the paint or make lines in it with pointed sticks – they have even been known to burn it or treat it with chemicals. The artist feels free to use the paint any way he can to get the effect he wants.

Changes

Artists have used oil paint because it can do many things. Most pictures are built up in layers, some you can see through and some you cannot. Each layer *changes* what went before until the artist achieves what he wants. Often, as a painting gets old, the colours become more transparent and the changes show through. These are sometimes called *pentimenti*, an Italian word. You can learn a great deal of what an artist was thinking about or trying to do from looking at these changes.

An example of such changes can be seen in 'Harvest Scene, Afternoon' by G. R. Lewis. The figure of a man sitting on a sheaf of corn, which the artist painted out, is now plainly visible just to the left of the centre of the painting. Lewis also seems to have added as an afterthought the tall figure of a man on the left because you can see corn stubble showing through his breeches above the knee. Most of the other figures are painted directly on to the canvas and not over finished bits of landscape. These changes, together with other small ones have the effect that the group of figures which was closed on the right and open on the left is now closed on the left and open on the right. The group is open, therefore, towards the wide and distant landscape. This means that the group of farm labourers does not turn away from the fields and the view. But neither do they gaze at the landscape like tourists or holiday makers. They seem to belong to it – it is where they work. Certainly the early nineteenth century, when this picture was painted, was a period when people began to see more clearly the importance and value of work in the countryside. The changes made by the artist seem to reflect this new awareness.

G.R. Lewis, **Harvest Scene, Afternoon** *c.* 1815

Original position of figures shown in red

Studies and Sketches

At all times painters and sculptors have made sketches and studies as well as the finished paintings that are generally intended to be exhibited in public. Sometimes these are on the same canvas as the finished painting and remain part of it or are covered up, but often they are on separate bits of paper, canvases or panels. They may be themselves drawings, watercolours, paintings or notes in words or numbers.

Such studies have a number of different uses. For example, they can be records of information – the shape of a face, a mountain or any object that the artist may eventually need for a particular picture. Modern artists often use photographs for this purpose as Hockney did (p. 54). In particular sketches or photographs can be used as records of something that is passing by rapidly or changing. Here are some other reasons for making studies and sketches:

■ Studies can be ways of working out the arrangement of the things which are to go into a picture (see the page entitled 'Composition' p. 70).

■ They can be experiments, ways of finding out how to get the effect of something the artist has seen, like the shine of dew on grass or of ripples on water.

■ They can be a way of practising a skill just as a musician practises on an instrument.

■ They can be a way of showing someone who may want to buy a large finished painting or sculpture what it will look like.

Constable is an artist who made studies for several of these purposes and many others.

Pencil and chalk study by Copley for 'The Death of Major Peirson' *c.*1783

Oil sketch by Constable for 'Flatford Mill'

Prints

Besides paintings and sculpture, the Tate Gallery also has a large collection of artists' prints. These are different from the ordinary reproduction prints because, usually, they have been made from images created on the printing surface by the artist in person.

There are four principal kinds of printing surfaces used both by artists and trade printers:

Relief is like potato or lino cuts in which the image area stands above and clear of the surrounding surface. Ink is applied with a roller before paper is pressed to the surface from which the image is transferred.

Intaglio (In-TALLY-o) etching or engraving where the artist creates his image by making grooves in a thin flat plate, usually of copper. The grooves are either 'bitten in' with nitric acid (etched) or cut with a sharp pointed tool (engraved). The grooves are then filled with stiff ink and the surrounding surfaces carefully wiped clean of the surplus. Dampened (and therefore softened) paper is laid over the plate and they are then run between powerful rollers under springy woollen blankets. This forces the paper into the lines to pick up the ink. Each impression requires fresh inking.

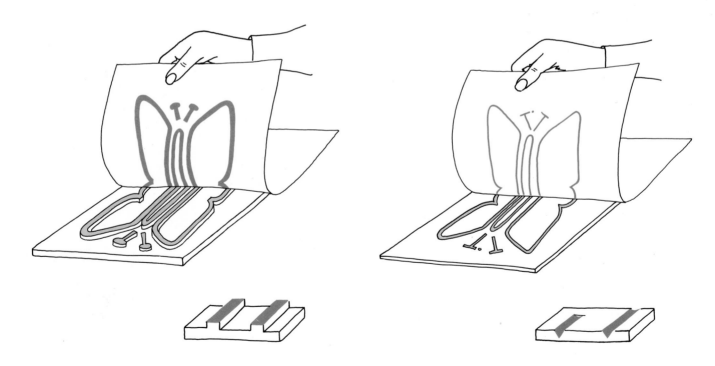

Lithography relies on the natural antipathy of grease and water. The artist draws with a greasy crayon on the fine-grained surface of a specially prepared limestone block or zinc plate. The surface is then wiped with water which is repelled by the greasy image, but it remains on the surrounding areas. Ink is then applied with a roller – the greasy image accepts it readily, but it fails to stick to the non-printing area because of the water it carries. The paper is then laid on to the surface and the scraping pressure of a long-edged blade forces it into a contact sufficient to pick up the ink. Each impression requires fresh inking.

Silk Screen is a form of stencil through which paint or ink can be squeezed on to the paper. The fine mesh of the screen is open enough to let the ink through but supports a detailed design that can be glued or photographed on to it. This prevents the ink passing through and the image will be those parts not blocked in this way.

In most kinds of printing, only one colour is used at a time. But if the artist wants several colours he can print them one after the other using a different plate or screen each time.

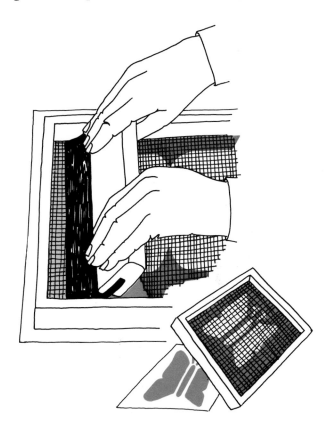

The antipathy of grease and water – the principle on which lithography is based

Space and Dimensions

A point like this · if it is very small, has very nearly no dimensions, it has almost no length, width or depth and occupies almost no space. Its main function is to mark a particular place. All the illustrations in this book are made up of tiny dots of colour. The purpose of each dot is simply to mark one place on the page with its own colour. Some paintings have been made in this way.

Think of making a dot on a sheet of paper with a sharp pencil. Now think of making another dot and, without lifting the pencil, drawing it across the paper. Of course you would have made a line. A line is like a moving dot. A straight line has length and direction but almost no width. It has one dimension. In paintings and especially drawings, a line sometimes represents a thing which is long and thin like a hair or piece of string. More often it is used to separate one thing from another: a head from the space round it; it defines a shape. When used like this it is called an outline. A line can also show movement or the direction in which something is going as in the work by Richard Long (p. 57).

In a painting the colour is usually put on with a brush and covers an area which is wide as well as long; it has two dimensions. The canvas or board on which you paint also has length and width but is flat and so one can say that the picture itself has only two dimensions, while a sculpture has depth as well and has three dimensions.

But pictures often represent objects in the world which have depth or distance. The skill of the painter has, for a long time, been concerned with the use of the two dimensions of the picture

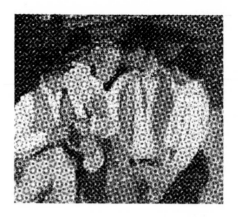

and with the three dimensions of the world he creates or suggests to us by it. Here are some of the ways he can make his flat picture represent a world in three dimensions:

■ If he makes marks that form a pattern which we recognise as like something we know in the world, we can easily fill in what is not there: two dots and two lines in a circle are a face and our imagination at once gives us the whole head.

■ If one shape seems to overlap another, we see that one is in front of the other.

■ Shading can make a circle look like a ball and a shadow beneath it can show you that it's on a surface.

■ If you know how big a thing is, its size in relation to other things in the picture tells you how far away it is – the smaller it is the further away it seems.

■ If the lines with which you draw something converge (that is they are closer together at one end than the other), they also suggest that it is slanting back into the distance. This effect is called perspective. An artist may emphasise the effect by putting his figure or objects on a patterned floor, see Hogarth p. 7, Alma-Tadema p. 25.

Changes of colour can also suggest distance. Painters have often shown how mountains far away look bluish. Finally, artists may make things which are close up look sharply defined while those that are to be a long way away slightly blurred or have less detail, see Lewis p. 60, Constable p. 17 and Derain p. 27.

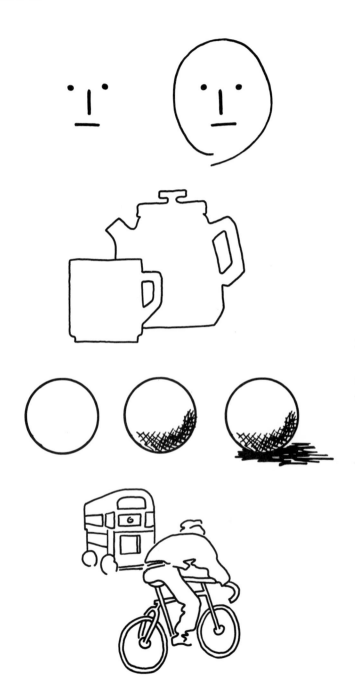

Colour

Paintings are really all colour. Even black and white are colours, and the canvas, paper or board on which the painting is made also has colour. Your eye can tell the difference between enormous numbers of colours, far, far more than we have names for. They are different from one another in three different ways which are called, *hue*: red, orange, yellow, etc., *intensity*: whether the colour is strong or weak, clear or greyish and *brightness*: which is the strength of the coloured light reflected by the paint. Black, for example, reflects little light, white a lot. The eye sees some colours more brightly than others so that yellow looks brighter than blue. But what you can do with colour in paintings is affected by other things.

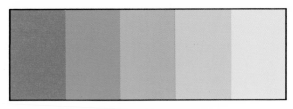

Reducing brightness, or luminosity, of colour

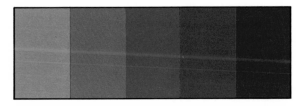

Reducing intensity, purity, or saturation, of colour

The brightness and hue of paints are affected by the light you see them in, whether it is strong or weak and whether it is warm like candlelight or cold like fluorescent tubes.

In the past some colours (hues) were available in a form that was strong and permanent and could be made into paint while others were not and had to be mixed. These would not be so intense. For example, there was a very strong blue and good reds while the yellows were rather brownish and there was no strong green or purple. Green was often made by mixing a strong blue and a weak yellow so in old paintings it is generally dull and brownish. About 150 years ago chemists began to discover and make new colours so that artists were able to paint very strong yellows, greens and purples which you see in Pre-Raphaelite paintings and in many modern

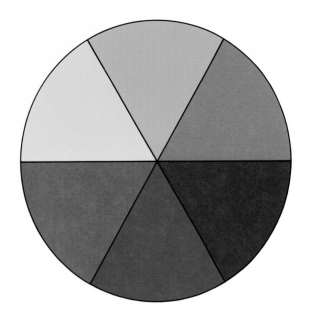

ones. Compare the colours in the Derain p. 27 to those in the Constable p. 17.

When one strong colour is put next to another it may seem to come out in front of it or to sink behind it so colour too can be used to make an effect of space.

 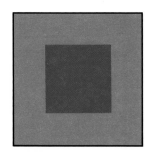

Colour can certainly affect the way you feel. People have often compared it to the sounds of music for this reason.

Sometimes colours seem to have this effect because of what they make you think of, red as blood, blue as a summer sky, green as grass, brown as wood, etc. But it is possible that sometimes the effect may be because of something in the brain which responds automatically to different colours. Perhaps the fact that we see red as warm and blue as cold is like this rather than because we associate them with fire and ice.

Some abstract pictures use these effects of colour without relating them to any objects that you can see in the world around you (Rothko p. 47, Stella p. 51). But artists who are making a picture of people or things that you might see, use colour in the same way by choosing objects

or by imagining them with the colours they need. In the Hogarth, the 'practical' boy is in brown.

Sometimes an artist gets a strong effect by exaggerating natural colours, by simplifying them or by painting a thing in a quite unexpected colour (Derain p. 27).

The colours in painting affect one another. For example, green and red next to each other make the other much stronger while red and brown do not. A very large part of the skill of a painter is in being able to use colour to get the effects he wants. Notice the spots of red in the Constable which make the large areas of green look greener. (p. 17).

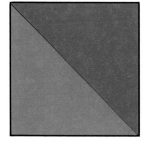 

Scale

The size of a picture can be a very important part of it. This is something that is difficult to show in a book like this where the reproductions are quite similar in size, and never very large, while the original paintings can sometimes be enormous.

Some pictures have been large because they formed part of the decoration of large rooms, or because they were a demonstration of the riches, power and ambition of their owners, like large cars today, or because they had to include a great deal of detail. But there are other reasons. One of these is connected with the fact that a picture is an object in the real world so that a painter may want to represent a person in a portrait in actual size or even enlarged so as to suggest an heroic or threatening dominance.

The size or scale of a picture is especially important when it is abstract, since there is nothing represented in the picture which has its own size that you recognise, such as a person. Very large pictures can be like whole walls of rooms and are part of the space you are in while medium sized ones are like furniture, small ones like objects you can handle and very small ones are like jewellery you can wear.

Size within a picture or sculpture is, of course, also very significant. It is often connected to the importance a painter attaches to a particular figure or object. This can be seen very clearly in paintings by children but it is also true of some of the most professional art. Sometimes, however, a painter will make the most important part of a picture very small. This may be because he wants to draw attention to its smallness or loneliness but it may also be a means of getting you to search

for the thing so that when you eventually find it it becomes more precious, like Queen Mab in 'The Fairy Feller's Master Stroke' p. 23.

Movement

Gino Severini, **Suburban Train arriving at Paris** 1915

Paintings and sculptures have, for thousands of years, represented a world in which things are always moving while they remain still themselves. Many artists, aware of this contradiction, have kept movement to a minimum but the problem is very important to an artist when he is illustrating a story or when he is representing something whose most obvious purpose is to move, like a train or racehorse.

The effect of movement can be given by the composition as a whole. But if you look at individual figures of people or animals in pictures you often see them apparently frozen in the act of doing something. They may be frozen in a position which conveys movement, because it would be impossible to remain like that, but more usually they are represented at the extreme point of some action. These positions become conventions in art and sometimes have very little relation to what actually happens.

An example is the running horse or dog which for a long time was represented with its legs stretched out to the front and behind at the same time. This seemed to suggest great energy and speed until the camera showed that a dog in fact never gets into this position. When photography did appear it made gestures of this kind look old fashioned and introduced several new ways of representing movement, especially blurring and multiple images.

In the twentieth century many artists have turned against devices that give an illusion or suggestion of movement, if they need action, they have made the work of art itself move or change. This kind of art is called kinetic. It has generally been abstract and is meant to give pleasure or to affect people in other ways by the use of movement itself. More recently, when artists have wanted to present a kind of story or succession of happenings they have used film or video, which were invented for the purpose, or have taken to performing themselves.

J.N. Sartorius, **The Earl of Darlington foxhunting with the Raby Pack: Full Cry** 1804 (detail)

Sir Alfred Munnings, **Their Majesties' return from Ascot** 1925 (detail)

Composition

This word refers to the space in the picture or sculpture itself and the way the parts of it are arranged together in it. In a painting it refers to the arrangement on a *flat* surface like a canvas although this cannot be separated from the arrangement in the imaginary space that a painter may create. There are almost as many kinds of composition as pictures that have been painted and there are no kinds of composition that are in themselves bad or good. An artist chooses one that gives him the effects he wants.

In a portrait of a person like the Gainsborough p. 11, the important and interesting bit, the head, is nearly always near the optical centre. The main point of the picture is to show what the person looked like.

The picture by Dadd on p. 23 shows the effect of scattering details all over the picture in an almost even manner. Pollock's 'Number 23' shows the same thing in an abstract picture. But

Jackson Pollock, **Number 23** 1948

you can see how different is the effect of concentrating them in one place as they are in the Blake (p. 15). One seems to create a mood the other to focus attention on a particular event.

In the painting by Stubbs (p. 9) three dark horses on the left are balanced by the single white horse which is near the centre but stands out more strongly. The large upright tree is balanced by the interest of the distant bright landscape, so that objects are balanced which are different from one another. The same is true in the picture by Constable (p. 17) and is the most usual type of composition. You can also see it in the abstract picture by Mondrian (p. 33). In the Rothko (p. 47) on the other hand the two sides are the same – it is symmetrical. The picture by Copley (p. 13) is also fairly symmetrical with a large group in the middle then a gap on either side with large figures at the edges.

The Nash (p. 43) runs all one way to create a feeling that the wrecked planes go on forever. But extremely unbalanced works are very rare. Here are some other compositional types:

In the Alma-Tadema (p. 25), the most interesting parts are at the edges and there is a space in the middle; in the Blake (p. 15) they are in the middle with space all around. In the Dali (p. 39) and the Turner (p. 19) everything is linked together by curving lines. In the Cholmondeley portraits (p. 5) and Lowry (p. 45) the parts of the picture are separated from one another.

In the Stella (p. 51) and the Cholmondeley portraits the parts are similar to one another, while Constable has tried to make as many differences as he can – people standing, sitting and lying, resting and working, fields in sunlight and in shadow, land and water and so on.

The shape of the picture, too, is important. Usually the artist chooses a shape that seems to fit what is in it, landscapes are usually horizontal, portraits vertical but sometimes he chooses a shape which is unexpected, like Richard Smith in his painting 'Vista'.

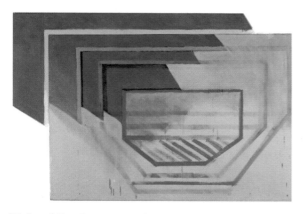

Richard Smith, **Vista** 1963

Expression and Style

I have often described the effect of painting in a certain way. This is what is sometimes called 'expression' sometimes 'style'. An artist tells as much by *how* he paints as *what* he paints just as you do with your voice when you talk. There is no limit to the effects artists can get but here are some more examples.

A way in which pictures can be different from each other is shown by comparing the Hockney (p. 55) with the Gainsborough (p. 11). The Hockney is like a photograph in sharp focus. The shapes have clear-cut edges and the surfaces seem quite smooth. The other is rough and does not have sharp outlines. You can easily see the marks made by the artist's brush.

Generally, pictures like the Hockney seem careful and thoughtful. While others seem energetic and full of strong feeling. Artists who are trying to suggest that something is perfect or permanent will often paint in the exact and clear manner while artists who want to suggest conflict and change will work in the other way. However, an artist like Blake may reinforce the sense of energy in his picture by using precise shapes and lines which are themselves very strong.

The style or way in which a picture is painted may also tell you something about the artist's attitude to people and things. For example, pictures which are very clearly painted in bright colours and with simple shapes often represent beautiful heroic people. They seem to represent the world as it *ought* to be. Other artists have emphasised details or have painted commonplace or ugly subjects with strong shadows and rough outlines so that they seem to be representing the world as it *is* with all its faults rather than the world as it ought to be.

Some artists have tried to get the effect of the changing colour on the surface of things and even show how, in certain lights, the boundary between one thing and another is not distinct. These artists may be trying to get the effect not of how the world really is, which involves thought and knowledge, but simply of what it *looked like* at a particular moment, as Monet did.

Still others, by using unexpected shapes and colours may be trying to show none of these things but instead to try to show how they themselves *felt* about things.

The choice of the subject of a picture is an effective part of its expression or style. Some artists regularly choose violent themes, gales or battles, while others choose scenes of beauty and peace. Artists who usually paint animals may paint in a different way and expect a different response to those who paint houses. They use these objects to get different effects and it is the effect not the object that is important to them.

Artists paint abstract pictures or make abstract sculptures because they can get effects which they can not get if they are making works of art which look like objects or scenes in the world. They will therefore cheerfully abandon the effects that depend on our recognising the subject so as to bring to the work of art the feeling we usually connect with that subject.

However, the way an artist paints as well as what he paints is affected not only by his own personality and ideas but by the customs of the age in which he lives and by the conditions of his work. People who buy pictures may insist on a

Claude Monet, **Poplars on the Epte** 1890

certain subject – when they commission a portrait for example – but it may be just that in certain periods people have wanted certain kinds of pictures. In the middle of the nineteenth century for example there was a great demand for pictures of cattle and sheep. Nowadays there are people who want to buy only what they think is the latest style – the subject matters much less. An artist therefore both creates new visions and reflects those of his day.